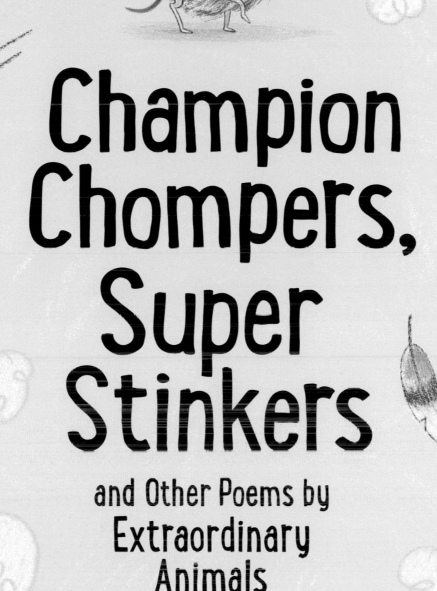

Champion Chompers, Super Stinkers

and Other Poems by Extraordinary Animals

Written by Linda Ashman

Illustrated by Aparna Varma

KIDS CAN PRESS

To my extraordinary friends,
Lillian and Caroline — L.A.

For the furriest fluffy, Comet — A.V.

Published in Canada and the U.S. by Kids Can Press Ltd.
25 Dockside Drive, Toronto, ON M5A 0B5

Kids Can Press is a Corus Entertainment Inc. company
www.kidscanpress.com

The artwork in this book was rendered digitally.
The text is set in Stone Informal.

Edited by Yasemin Uçar and Kathleen Keenan
Designed by Barb Kelly

Printed and bound in Malaysia in 10/2022

CM 23 0 9 8 7 6 5 4 3 2 1

Library and Archives Canada Cataloguing in Publication

Title: Champion chompers, super stinkers and other poems by extraordinary animals / written by Linda Ashman ; illustrated by Aparna Varma.
Names: Ashman, Linda, author. | Varma, Aparna, illustrator.
Description: Includes poems and factual information about animals, structured in a guessing game format.
Identifiers: Canadiana 20220229929 | ISBN 9781525303500 (hardcover)
Subjects: LCSH: Animal behavior — Juvenile literature. | LCSH: Animals — Juvenile literature. | LCSH: Animal behavior — Juvenile poetry. | LCSH: Animals — Juvenile poetry. | LCSH: Biodiversity — Juvenile literature. | LCSH: Guessing games — Juvenile literature. | LCGFT: Riddles.
Classification: LCC QL751.5 .A75 2023 | DDC j591.5 — dc23

Kids Can Press gratefully acknowledges that the land on which our office is located is the traditional territory of many nations, including the Mississaugas of the Credit, the Anishnabeg, the Chippewa, the Haudenosaunee and the Wendat peoples, and is now home to many diverse First Nations, Inuit and Métis peoples.

We thank the Government of Ontario, through Ontario Creates; the Ontario Arts Council; the Canada Council for the Arts; and the Government of Canada for supporting our publishing activity.

CONTENTS

Calling all contestants!
Think you're tops?
The most?
The best?

Are you bigger ...
taller ...
faster ...
smaller ...
STRONGER than the rest?

We have ways to test and measure —
Speed, endurance, skills and size.
Who's the winner?

Let's get started.
Time to see who takes first prize.

EAT MY DUST

I'm designed for lightning speed —

Just look at this physique:

Limber spine,

Impressive stride,

I'm **long** and **strong** and **sleek**.

SO — you think you'd beat me in a race?

Well, here's a hint:

Make sure that it's a marathon —

You'll never win a sprint.

Cheetah

With their lean bodies, long stride and sharp claws for traction, cheetahs are designed to be *fast*. In fact, they're the fastest animal on land. When chasing prey, they can exceed speeds of 110 km (70 mi.) per hour — about the rate of cars on a highway. But using so much energy takes its toll. Cheetahs wear out quickly and need time to rest before they eat their meal — or try again (their hunt is successful only about half the time).

CATCH ME IF YOU CAN

When you're seen as someone's dinner,

It's risky to be slow.

But I can outrun anyone.

Just watch me:

Ready?

GO!

Certain cats are quicker —

They're good for one short burst.

But when the race is longer,

I will *always* come in first.

Pronghorn

Pronghorn are native to North America, so they're not likely to race against any cheetahs. But if given the chance, and a brief head start, they'd probably outrun them. These sleek creatures are built for running, with slender, long-striding legs, padded hooves for shock absorption, and oversized hearts and lungs for pumping blood and carrying oxygen to muscles. They're fast, too, exceeding rates of 80 km (50 mi.) per hour. And unlike cheetahs, they can maintain those high speeds across long distances — which is a huge advantage when bobcats, wolves, coyotes and other predators come looking for a pronghorn picnic.

BLURRED BIRD

In terms of speed, it's guaranteed —
There is no better show.
I start my flight from a towering height,
then ...

WHOOOSH!

Look out below!

Peregrine Falcon

In pursuit of their prey — typically birds or bats — peregrine falcons start from a high vantage point, then drop like a missile toward their target. In this steep dive, or stoop, they can reach speeds of 320 km (200 mi.) per hour, making them not just the fastest flyers but also the speediest animals on Earth.

SLOWPOKE

Although I know
I'm *very* slow
(the pokiest around),

I take first prize,

Endurance-wise,

For time spent upside down.

SLOWEST Mammal

Three-Toed Sloth

Imagine spending your days hanging from a tree branch, mostly sleeping, with occasional breaks for eating. That's the life of the three-toed sloth. With their long claws and strong grip, they're perfectly suited to hanging around. They spend so much time in trees, and move so little, that algae grow on their fur. The algae's greenish tinge provides camouflage in the rain forest, helping the sloth hide from predators.

FREQUENT FLYER

No one can match my amazing migration,

My stamina, strength and superb navigation.

How do I manage this epic commute,

Crossing the globe on my pole-to-pole route?

Returning again without tour guide or map?

That's easy:

I *flap*...

and I *flap*...

and I *flap*...

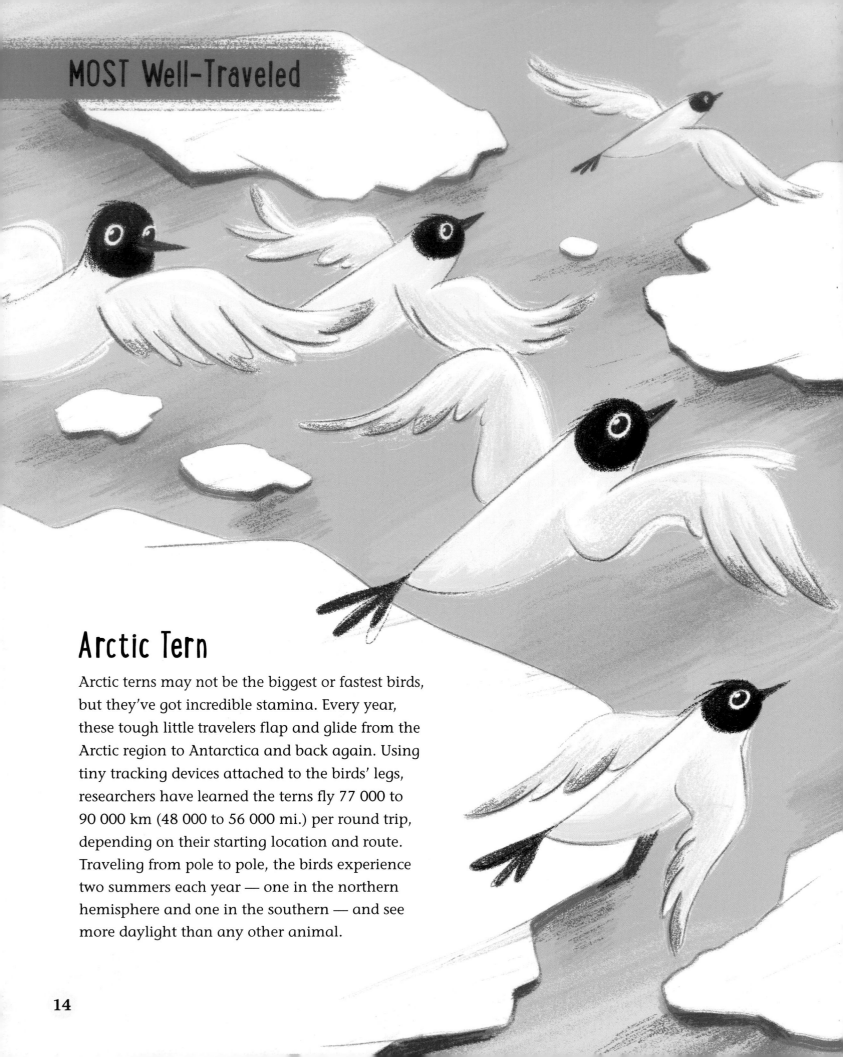

Arctic Tern

Arctic terns may not be the biggest or fastest birds, but they've got incredible stamina. Every year, these tough little travelers flap and glide from the Arctic region to Antarctica and back again. Using tiny tracking devices attached to the birds' legs, researchers have learned the terns fly 77 000 to 90 000 km (48 000 to 56 000 mi.) per round trip, depending on their starting location and route. Traveling from pole to pole, the birds experience two summers each year — one in the northern hemisphere and one in the southern — and see more daylight than any other animal.

WHO TURNED OFF THE LIGHTS?

Deep **below** the ocean waves,

Far from sandy beaches —

I swim in frigid darkness

Where the sunlight never **reaches.**

DEEPEST-DWELLING Fish

Snailfish

Life isn't easy in the farthest depths of the ocean. It's freezing cold and pitch black, and the weight of all that water creates intense pressure. Yet 8 km (5 mi.) below the ocean's surface, scientists have discovered a new species of snailfish — nicknamed the "ghost fish" for its translucent appearance — that has managed to survive in this harsh environment. What's the secret to its success? Like other deep-dwelling sea creatures, the snailfish has high levels of a special chemical (trimethylamine oxide or TMAO) that prevents its cell walls from being crushed by the weight of the water. TMAO also gives fish their distinctive odor, so the deepest-dwelling creatures are also the fishiest-smelling!

AERIE ARCHITECT

No dreary cave,

No teensy cup,

No rocky shore will do.

I want the best:
A *spacious* nest

And dazzling penthouse view.

Bald Eagle

In choosing their home sites, bald eagles look for
locations high in a tall tree near water. It needs to be
a sturdy tree, because the eagle's nest, or aerie, is *big*.
Built by the male and female — who mate for life — the
nest is constructed of branches and sticks woven together
with softer materials such as grass, moss, cornstalks
and feathers. The pair typically remodels the aerie
each year, making it even bigger. The largest nest
on record was 2.9 m (9.5 ft.) wide, 6 m (20 ft.)
deep and weighed about 2 t (4400 lb.),
more than four grand pianos.

TOOTHY TOOLS

I built this sturdy lodge

Without cement or brick.

No chain saw, drill or chisel —

My incisors do the trick:

stripping,
felling,
gnawing,
towing.

Luckily, my teeth keep growing.

19

North American Beaver

Beavers are impressive landscape designers and engineers. They build and maintain dams, create ponds and canal systems and construct homes, or lodges, using branches and logs plastered together with mud. They do much of this work — cutting down trees, gnawing through branches and transporting building materials — using their teeth, particularly their four prominent and distinctively orange-colored incisors. Fortunately, a beaver's teeth keep growing throughout its life, so these all-purpose tools don't wear out.

MARINE MICHELANGELO

My work's precise, exhausting, slow —

**Back and forth,
To and fro —**

Sculpting sand on a massive scale,

Using just my fins and tail.

Day in, day out,

I cannot cease.

Behold: my deep-sea **masterpiece!**

Few will see my genius,

But that is not my goal.

I must create — it is my fate:

I have an artist's soul.

BEST Undersea Artist

White-Spotted Puffer Fish

For many years, scuba divers near Japan were puzzled by circular patterns they observed on the seafloor. In 2011, scientists finally discovered the source of these mysterious works of art: the white-spotted puffer fish, a small and otherwise unremarkable fellow. Thanks to underwater filming, we're able to watch these artists in action. For longer than a week, they work nonstop to create amazing circular designs of hills and valleys more than 20 times their body size, decorated with bits of coral and seashells. The male puffer fish does all this hard work to attract a mate. When he succeeds, the female lays her eggs at the center of the circle and swims away, leaving the artist to care for them alone.

LAP HAPPY

Feeble eyesight. Toothless jaws.

But see this snout?

This tongue?

These claws?

I'm perfectly built for lapping up ants.

SLURP!

So delicious.

They don't stand a chance.

Giant Anteater

If you ate mostly ants and termites — say, about 30 000 each day — you'd want a tongue like a giant anteater's. It's about half a meter (1.6 ft.) long, looks something like a skinny snake and is covered in sticky saliva. After breaking open an ant mound with its powerful claws, the anteater rapidly flicks its tongue inside to lap up thousands of ants before moving on to another mound.

I WARNED YOU!

Note this pose,

This hood,

This **hiss** —

My meaning's loud and clear.

It's not *Let's play!*

Or *Oh*, *please stay.*

It's *SCRAM! Get outta here.*

King Cobra

Yes, king cobras are long, nearly 5.5 m (18 ft.) in some cases, but they're quite distinctive in other ways, too. When threatened, they can lift their heads as high as 1.8 m (6 ft.), flare out their famous hoods and hiss loudly. All of this is their way of saying, "Go away, or I'll bite you!" Since such a bite can be deadly — the king cobra's venom is powerful enough to kill an elephant — it's best to heed the warning and leave it alone.

CHAMPION CHOMPER

I'm not picky:

Furred or feathered,

Sleek or scaly,

Young or weathered.

I'm not deterred by

Shape or size,

But wait, submerged,

And then ...

SURPRISE!

I'm quiet and patient,

Stealthy and sly.

I greet with a

SNAP!

Then it's

CRUNCH CRUNCH

Goodbye.

Saltwater Crocodile

The saltwater crocodile is a real champ when it comes to chomping. The croc's bite is more powerful than a car-crushing machine and nearly four times stronger than a grizzly bear's. Although saltwater crocodiles are big — the largest reptiles in the world — they're very good at hiding. They lurk in the water, partly submerged, until an animal — any animal! — ventures within snapping distance. Look out!

SUPER STINKERS

I really stink.

Oh, yeah? Me, too!

I stink the *most*.

No way. *I* do.

See this goo that I excrete?

It reeks! This stuff is tough to beat.

A liquid? That can't top my spray.

Folks smell ME from far away.

Just come closer.

Take a whiff.

Okay — I'll spray then.

Ready?

Sniff!

WHOA — my nose!

OUCH — my eyes!

I guess you're right —
YOU win first prize!

How do you rank stinkiness? Scientists can identify the chemical compounds that contribute to the offensive odors animals (including humans) produce, but who decides which animal smells the worst? The sniffer! So take a whiff — you be the judge!

EURASIAN HOOPOE

The Eurasian hoopoe is a beautiful bird with an eye-catching crown of feathers — and some repulsive habits. During egg-laying season, the female hoopoe produces a foul-smelling brown liquid from a gland beneath her tail. She spreads this liquid all over her feathers and eggs. Within days of hatching, her nestlings are making the same putrid goop. But that's not all: when predators approach the nest, the little stinkers shoot poop to scare them off. Hoopoes also leave their droppings in the nest — all of which makes for one nasty-smelling home.

and STRIPED SKUNK

The striped skunk is famous for its smelly defense mechanism: two small nozzles located under its tail. When threatened, the skunk directs its back end toward the menace and blasts a wretched-smelling liquid that can hit a target about 3 m (10 ft.) away. The powerful spray can sting the eyes and cling to skin, fur and clothing for days. With a little breeze, the scent carries quite a distance. So even if they've never encountered the critter tail-to-face, lots of North Americans recognize the distinctive funk of a stressed-out skunk.

SPEED EATER

I might seem small and puny,

But here's my claim to fame:

Each day, I eat more than I weigh —

Bet you can't say the same.

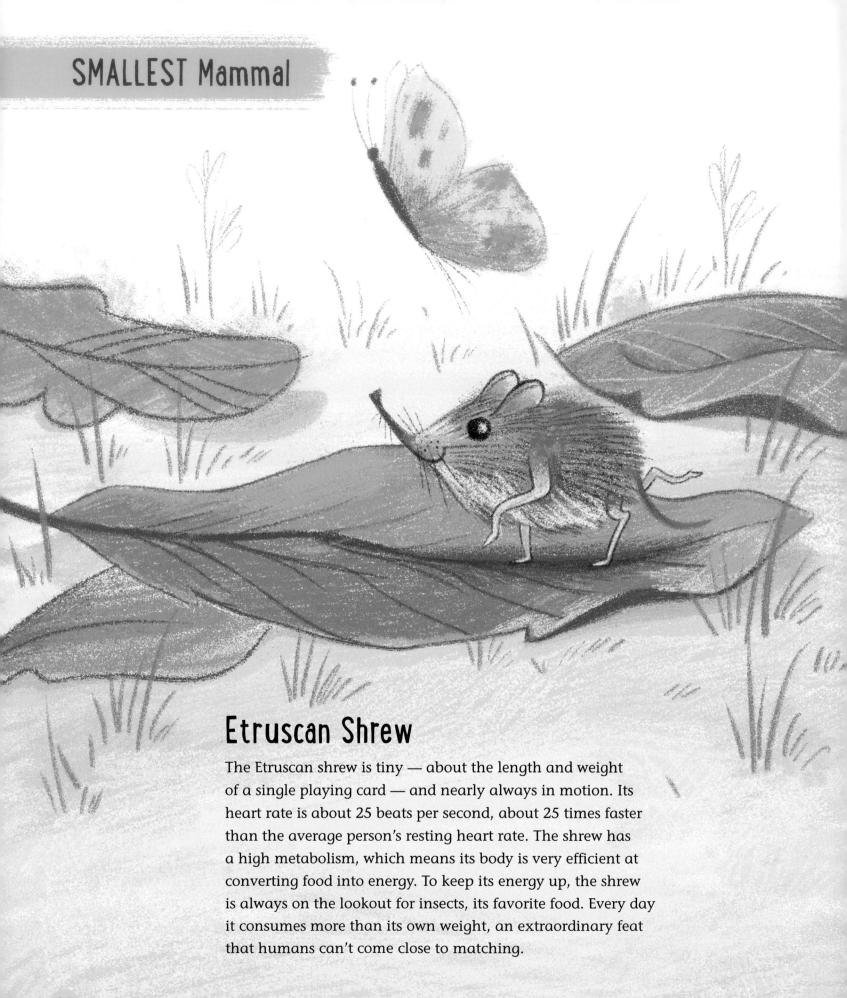

Etruscan Shrew

The Etruscan shrew is tiny — about the length and weight of a single playing card — and nearly always in motion. Its heart rate is about 25 beats per second, about 25 times faster than the average person's resting heart rate. The shrew has a high metabolism, which means its body is very efficient at converting food into energy. To keep its energy up, the shrew is always on the lookout for insects, its favorite food. Every day it consumes more than its own weight, an extraordinary feat that humans can't come close to matching.

ONE OF A KIND

Look at this pattern, exclusively mine.

My tail fringe and eyelashes? Simply divine.

This long, slender neck.

Superior height.

You say I'm exquisite?

My goodness —

You're right!

Giraffe

Picture three tall grown-ups standing on one another's shoulders — that's about the height of a typical giraffe. A giraffe's legs and neck alone are each about 1.8 m (6 ft.) tall. But these lanky creatures are remarkable in many ways besides their size. Despite those gangly legs, they can be quite fast, reaching speeds of 56 km (35 mi.) per hour. Their powerful kick can scare off lions and other dangerous predators. And have you ever noticed the distinctive pattern on a giraffe's coat? Each one is unique, just like our fingerprints.

PRACTICALLY PERFECT

I'm tops for size,

For eyes and eggs.

The *fastest runner* on two legs.

Accomplished? Yes!

But I can't lie —

I really wish that I could *fly!*

Ostrich

The ostrich is extraordinary in many ways. Standing up to 2.8 m (9 ft.) high, it's the tallest bird, and at 130 kg (286 lb.), it's also the heaviest. But that's not all! Its eyes are 5 cm (2 in.) wide, the largest peepers of any land animal. Its eggs are the biggest, too, weighing 1.4 kg (3 lb.) each, about as much as two dozen chicken eggs. Plus, it's the fastest two-legged animal, reaching speeds of nearly 72 km (45 mi.) per hour. Yet this multiple-medal-winning bird is unable to fly — its wings are just too small to support its large body.

ALL I NEED IN ONE TRUNK

Yes, I'm colossal.

(My brain's giant, too.)

But check out this nose and all it can do:

shower, spray, drink, play,
snorkel, trumpet, dine;
Breathe, lift, grab, sniff—

What an ingenious design!

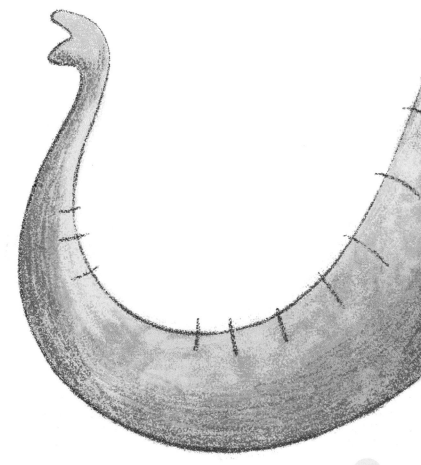

African Elephant

African elephants (as opposed to the smaller Asian elephant species) can exceed 3 m (10 ft.) in height and more than 6 t (7 tn.) in weight — about as hefty as four mid-sized cars. These elephants are also known for their intelligence and have the largest brain of any land animal (three times larger than human brains). But beyond their size and smarts, elephants have an amazingly versatile tool: their trunk! Among other functions, it's used like a nose for smelling and breathing, like an arm for moving and lifting, and like a hand for grabbing, holding and touching. An elephant can also use its trunk to suck up water (part way), then spray it into its mouth to drink or over its head like a shower. Very handy!

HEY, SMALL FRY!

I am ENORMOUS!

No one compares:

Not dinos

or elephants,

rhinos or bears.

Want to grow big

And weigh what I weigh?

Try eating krill — forty million a day.

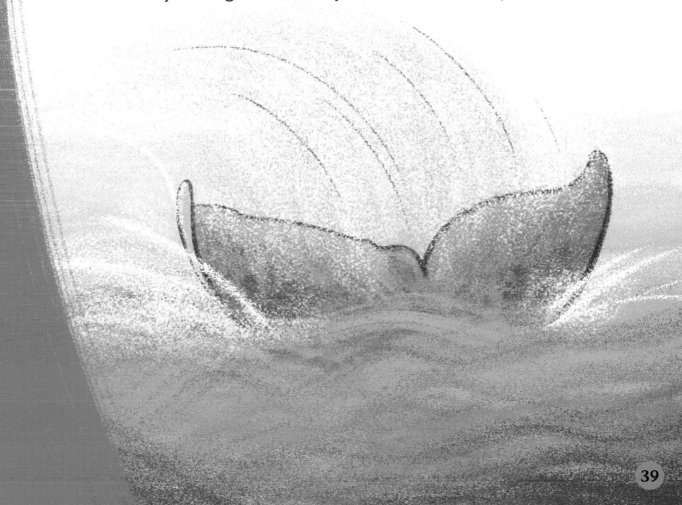

Blue Whale

Blue whales are the most massive animals to ever live, significantly outweighing even the biggest dinosaurs. Some blue whales reach 30 m (100 ft.) in length long and weigh more than 180 t (200 tn.). That's longer than ten surfboards stretched end to end and heavier than 25 elephants. It takes a lot of food to maintain that kind of size, especially when your preferred diet is a tiny shrimplike creature known as krill. During peak feeding season, blue whales consume some forty million krill — about 3.6 t (4 tn.) — every day. Yum!

THE SIMPLE LIFE

I've heard the world has changed some

Since I hatched here long ago.

But island life is quiet,

So I really wouldn't know.

The key to my longevity?

It's simple, like this poem:

Graze a little, sleep a lot,

Enjoy your cozy home.

Galápagos Tortoise

The giant tortoises of the Galápagos Islands include multiple species, each adapted to life on its particular island. These tortoises, the largest in the world, can measure 1.8 m (6 ft.) from head to tail and weigh more than 250 kg (551 lb.). Although they live longer than any other animal — in some cases more than 150 years — their lives aren't exactly what you'd call active. All told, a 150-year-old tortoise has spent about 100 years napping and the other 50 years mostly grazing on grass and other vegetation, soaking in the sun, wallowing in the mud and slowly (*very* slowly!) ambling around. Thanks to their sluggish metabolism and ability to store large amounts of water in their bladders, giant tortoises can even skip eating and drinking for up to a year.

Welcome back, contestants —
Take your prizes!
That was fun!
Many thanks to all who entered,
And congrats to those who've won.

We celebrate your blazing *speed*,
Your pole-to-pole migrations,
Your fine design and building skills,
Your undersea creations!

Hats off to your endurance,
Your strength and grit as well,
Your appetite, your fearsome bite,
Your *overwhelming* smell.

We've witnessed just a sampling
Of astounding feats and features.
Look around — we are surrounded
By extraordinary creatures!

Protecting Endangered Animals

We share our planet with incredible creatures, so many that we haven't come close to identifying all of them. Even so, scientists know that Earth's *biodiversity*, or the number and variety of animals, insects and plants within a particular environment, has been declining for some time due to human activity. When land is cleared for farming, new housing developments are built, rivers are polluted or climate changes affect a particular habitat, animals are displaced and may not survive.

Taken together, these and other changes have a big impact on biodiversity.

Why does biodiversity matter? A thriving ecosystem — whether it's a small tidal pool, a dry desert or the entire planet — depends on a varied mix of creatures, all living in balance. When one species is sick or disappears, it affects everything else within that ecosystem. In addition, some animals make important contributions to the planet that scientists are just beginning to understand. Take whales, for example. These amazing marine mammals help offset climate change by reducing the amount of heat-trapping carbon dioxide in the atmosphere. How?

Throughout their long lives, whales' bodies absorb carbon — and giant whales, like the blue whale, absorb even *more* carbon. When they die, they sink to the ocean floor, taking that carbon with them for deep-sea storage. In addition, whales emit "fecal plumes" (otherwise known as poop), which encourage the growth of phytoplankton, tiny marine algae that produce oxygen and absorb large amounts of carbon. Yet despite their carbon-capturing superpowers —

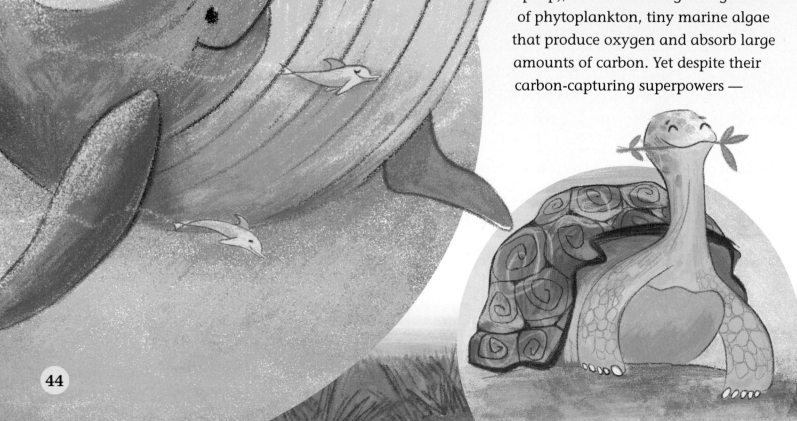

and their sheer awesomeness — many whale populations are at risk, and blue whales in particular are in danger of extinction.

Organizations such as the International Union for Conservation of Nature (IUCN) monitor that danger. The IUCN Red List of Threatened Species™ tracks the populations of thousands of animal and plant species worldwide, assigning each one a status based on threats to its survival, from Least Concern to Extinct. Many of the animals in this book — including king cobras, elephants, giraffes, cheetahs, giant anteaters and certain species of sloth and giant tortoise — are endangered, some critically so. Although we may never make it to the Galápagos Islands to see giant tortoises or meet giraffes and cheetahs in their natural habitat, we are all enriched by the existence of these remarkable creatures.

Several animals in this book were once close to extinction. Bald eagles, for example, suffered dramatic population declines in the mid-20th century due to habitat loss, hunting and use of the pesticide DDT, which caused their eggshells to thin and break before chicks hatched. By the early 1960s, there were fewer than five hundred nesting pairs. Thanks to protective measures and the banning of DDT, bald eagle populations have since recovered to healthy levels. That success story, and the return of other once-endangered animals like peregrine falcons, pronghorn and beavers, shows that government policies and our actions can help save animals from extinction. But we need to pay attention and recognize the value of all Earth's creatures — whether they're the biggest, tiniest, fastest, slowest or just somewhere in between.

To learn more about endangered animals and biodiversity, visit these websites:

Animal Diversity Web
https://animaldiversity.org/

IUCN Red List of Threatened Species™
https://www.iucnredlist.org/

National Wildlife Federation
https://www.nwf.org/

The Smithsonian's National Zoo
https://nationalzoo.si.edu/

World Wildlife Fund
https://www.worldwildlife.org/

About Measurements

It's not easy to measure a creature in motion, especially one that is dangerous, well-hidden or incredibly big. At a zoo, animals are weighed and measured much like we are when visiting a doctor — with a scale and some sort of ruler. Many can be trained to step on a scale (elephants, in particular, are very cooperative). But what about in the wild? How might you go about measuring a blue whale, for instance? Or the distance an arctic tern travels? Or the speed of a cheetah? It's not like you can put them on a race track and say, "Go!" Right?

Not quite — but scientists have managed to lure captive cheetahs with fake prey to see how fast they'll run after it. And skydivers have flown with trained peregrine falcons, dropping decoy bait to tempt the falcon into chasing it while they measure its speed. Scientists also use tracking devices attached to a cheetah's collar or a falcon's wing to determine speed, or clipped to a tiny band around an arctic tern's leg to follow its travels. Like all scientific inquiry, learning about animals begins with curiosity and lots of questions: Who's the biggest? The tiniest? The speediest? How can I find out?

I can fly!

About Mask Poems

Imagine you're a gigantic elephant, a deep-dwelling fish or a tiny shrew. What would it feel like to be such a creature: to move, to eat, to avoid being eaten? What would you want to say about yourself? In a mask poem (also known as a persona poem), we get to speak in the voice of someone or something we're not. We might write as if we're an animal, as in these poems, or something entirely different, like a raindrop or a thunderbolt. Just pretend you're something else — a butterfly, a button, a boat — and write about yourself. All it takes is a little imagination.

Recommended Reading

Elliott, David and Rob Dunlavey. *In the Woods*. Somerville, MA: Candlewick Press, 2020.

Florian, Douglas. *Ice! Poems about Polar Life*. New York: Holiday House, 2020.

Harrison, David L. and Kate Cosgrove. *The Dirt Book: Poems about Animals that Live Beneath Our Feet*. New York: Holiday House, 2021.

Hosford, Kate and Jennifer M. Potter. *A Songbird Dreams of Singing: Poems about Sleeping Animals*. Philadelphia: Running Press Kids, 2019.

Pincus, Meeg and Bao Luu. *Make Way for Animals: A World of Wildlife Crossings*. Minneapolis: Millbrook Press, 2022.

Poliquin, Rachel and Byron Eggenschwiler. *The Strangest Thing in the Sea: And Other Curious Creatures of the Deep*. Toronto: Kids Can Press, 2021.

Tuttle, Sarah Grace and Amy Schimler-Safford. *Hidden City: Poems of Urban Wildlife*. Grand Rapids, MI: Eerdmans Books for Young Readers, 2018.

Vande Griek, Susan and Mark Hoffman. *Hawks Kettle, Puffins Wheel: And Other Poems of Birds in Flight*. Toronto: Kids Can Press, 2019.

Glossary

biodiversity: all the different kinds of plants, animals and other organisms that exist in a particular place, whether it's a cave, a coral reef or the entire planet

camouflage: features, such as certain colors, patterns or shapes, that protect an animal from being seen by predators

ecosystem: a community of plants, animals and other living things that share the resources of a particular place and interact with and affect each other

endurance: the ability to do something difficult for a long period of time

frigid: extremely cold

hemisphere: one of the halves of Earth when it is divided from north to south or east to west

incisors: the front teeth, in humans and other mammals, used for biting and cutting

longevity: a long life span

metabolism: changes or reactions that happen in the cells of living things when their bodies take in food and turn it into energy

migration: the movement of animals from one region to another, often over long distances, typically prompted by a change in seasons

predator: an animal that kills other animals for food

prey: an animal that is killed by another animal for food

species: a group of living things that share similar characteristics

translucent: allowing some light to pass through, like frosted glass

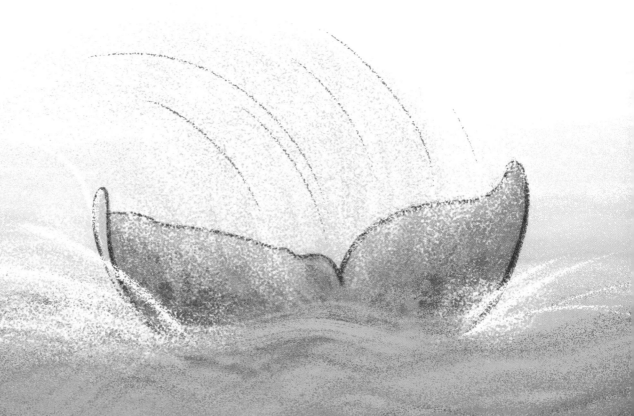